DREAM
WORLD

DREAM WORLD

David Hecker

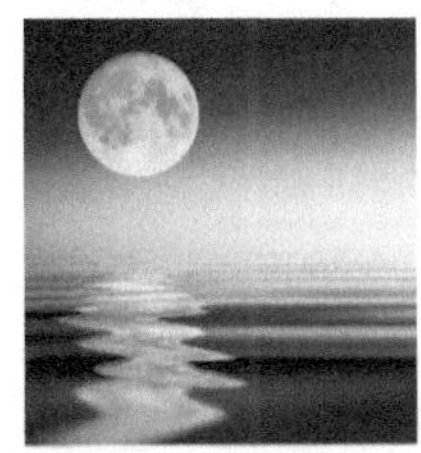

MoonPath Press

Poetry
ISBN 978-1-936657-77-3

Cover art: *The office of Hermann Hesse* by David Hecker
Author photo: by Jeffery Hecker

Book design by Tonya Namura, using Josifin Slab (display) and
Garamond Premier Pro (text)

MoonPath Press, an imprint of Concrete Wolf Poetry Series,
is dedicated to publishing the finest poets
living in the U.S. Pacific Northwest.

MoonPath Press
PO Box 445
Tillamook, OR 97141

MoonPathPress@gmail.com

http://MoonPathPress.com

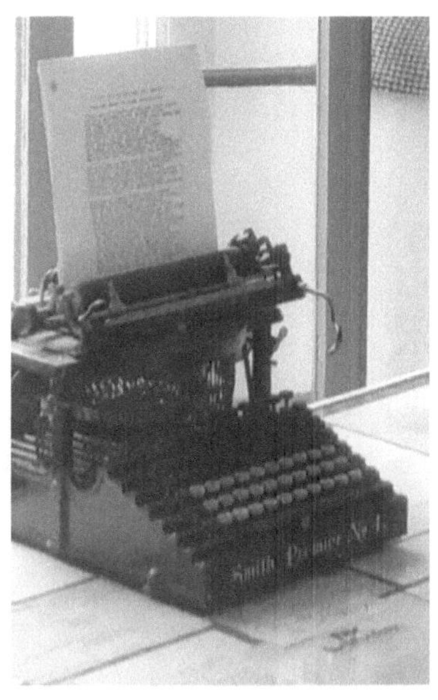

*All that we see or seem
Is but a dream within a dream.*

—Edgar Allen Poe

*But I, being poor, have only my dreams;
I have spread my dreams under your feet;
Tread softly because you tread on my dreams.*

—William Butler Yeats

Table of Contents

About This Collection   3

I Places

Earth Map   7
Grand Forest   8
Appaloosa Country (Fall 1982)   10
Grahams Island Cabin   11
Acoma Pueblo   13
Oxford, Mississippi   14
Dreamland Europe   15
Andalusia   20
Plaza de Bibarrambla   22
Antiquity Now   23
Whirling Dervishes   26
Qin Shi Huang   28
Three Gorges Dam   29
Chinese Busker in Shanghai   31
La Chascona, Neruda's Home   32
Literary Day in Dublin   35
Departure in 1893   38
Havamals for Traveling Iceland's Circle   40

II Dangers

Armed Forces Day Parade, 2004   45
658   47
Hitchhiking   48
Rescue   50
Dangers on the Slopes   52
Marriage Road   54
Dream or Reality   55
Precarious Waterfront   57
Vision   59
Squirrels   60
Barred Owl   61

Territory   62
Spider and Gnat   63
Revolutions   65
Tour Guide at Ushuaia   66

III   Voices

My Sister Veronica   71
Way of Life or Love?   73
Sandra's Vow   74
Solo Guitarist   76
Denise Levertov   77
Iambs for the New Age   79
The First Thread in Neruda's Life   80
Never Give Up   82
Time Off   84
Key West, Florida   85
In Memory of William Stafford   87
Ode to W.B. Yeats   88
Memorial   90
My Wall of Writers   91
Muse   92
Sculpting Words   93
My Wild Prairie Rose   94

Acknowledgments   97
About the Author   99

DREAM
WORLD

About This Collection

Most poets have aspirations and dreams that influence their writing of poems, according to quotations I've read in *Familiar Quotations*, edited by John Bartlett, and in *Writers Dreaming*, by editor Naomi Epel.

I had dreams about favorite writers and travelled to places where they lived and wrote. In America, I visited New York, Massachusetts, Florida, Mississippi, California, Oregon and Washington. The foreign countries I visited were Canada, Mexico, France, Italy, Austria, Germany, and then Chile, Ireland, Wales, England, Russia and Greece.

I also wrote poems about my dreams and aspirations to climb mountains, visit animals in their natural setting, explore political ideas, and pursue listening to voices of writers I've acknowledged as muses for my writing.

For added inspiration, I set up a wall of photographs of writers in my den next to my writing desk, printer, and computer.

The cover photo of this collection is of Hermann Hesse's office, taken at The Hermann Hesse Museum in Lugano, Italy when I visited. Hesse was a novelist and poet I greatly admire. I have read translations of many of his poems (from German into English) in a book titled *The Seasons of the Soul* (2011), edited by Ludwig Max Fischer, that contains many references to dreams in all parts of Hesse's 85-year long life.

I Places

The dream, like the dog, went on, travelled else-
where. Passed by the moment when everything
might have been changed. Passed by the moment
of knowing I wanted everything changed.
—Jane Hirshfield

If one advances confidently in the direction of his
dreams, and endeavors to live the life which he has
imagined, he will meet with the success unexpected
in common hours.
—Henry David Thoreau

Earth Map

Photograph of oldest known map
discovered by the American School
in Baghdad

Etched on a clay tablet,
mountains tumble down
both sides of a valley
where two rivers flow and meet.

Forty-five hundred years ago
in Northern Mesopotamia
travelers, eyes closed, ran
their fingers down the map,
feeling the journey ahead.

For no one should do more.

Sojourns demand uncertainties,
bad luck, good luck, ecstasies,
oddities, the truth or falsity of rumors,
and strange cuisine and customs.

Journeys offer respite from the familiar
and memories to relive at moments
of the inner eye, glimpses into
that far, yet near, past.

Grand Forest

Bush and meadow, field and tree,
Stand in their self-sufficient silence.
Each belonging wholly to itself.
Each deep in its own dream.
                —Hermann Hesse

I walk the trails of this forest,
grateful to have several hundred
acres of firs, cedar, pine and madrone
as well as blackberry bushes, holly,
nettles, fern, and a habitat for birds,
deer, raccoon, squirrel, and fox.

Soil under my feet, trek poles
in hands, I appreciate my peace
of mind with only an occasional
tap, tap, tap from a woodpecker
or *a-hoo, a-hoo, a-hoo* from an owl
or *caw, caw, caw* from a crow, giving
sounds of nature's music not noise.
There are no sidewalks, traffic lights,
pavement, thus no noise from engines,
or horns. There are no televisions,
computers, and I don't carry a cellphone,
so this place allows rejuvenation.

The sun shines on this late fall day.
It lights up and warms the trees, shrubs,
and turns frost to dew on the grass.
I forage in the bushes, eat a handful
of blackberries. Orange leaves
have fallen to the ground, though leaves
of evergreens remain on limbs.

I stop at a huge boulder with cairns set
up by fellow walkers and their children.
Thirty stacks with three to ten stones apiece
give witness to this site as a memorial
to this forest. I walk on, satisfied I am
not alone in my gratitude for nature's gifts.

Appaloosa Country (Fall 1982)

When I dream of horses,
I dream of the weight
In people's eyes.
           —Sally Albiso

Imagining Lewis and Clark's journey to this land, I drive up to this former kingdom to see where history had been made. Defended by Hells Canyon, the Blue Mountains, and forests of fir and pine, this high plateau country, former home of the proud Nez Perce nation and their magnificent horses, the Appaloosa, now has but a monument to Chief Joseph on the edge of Blue Lake. Chief Joseph and Looking Glass, forced to take flight with their people rather than be sequestered in the canyon below, chose to join Sitting Bull's band of Lakota in Canada. Theirs was an epic trek that ended in defeat, a betrayal for their generosity to Lewis and Clark.

At Blue Lake, I park near the statue of Chief Joseph, walk around it, admire its verdant location. There is only silence, not even a boat on the lake. The mountain peaks, just recently powdered with snow, reflect on the water's surface. I wonder how Bierstadt might have painted this scene or what music Paul Winter would have composed for it.

Back in my car, I motor past the monument out a circular drive, when from the corner of my eye, I see a figure standing near the statue of Chief Joseph. He is large and broad, a Native American with braided hair. As I slow to see better, the figure vanishes. Did I dream this image or is there a spirit left on the land as reminder of the vagaries of times past?

Grahams Island Cabin

I will arise and go now, and go to
Innisfree,
And a small cabin build there, of clay
And wattles made...
      —William Butler Yeats

This cabin once allowed you to retreat
from grandma, who twenty years later,
still lives in her five-bedroom house in town.
Now the cabin leans against a tree,
with broken glass windows,
warped siding and withered paint,
collapsing roof, and door hanging
by one hinge, the lower one.

Was it worth clearing forty acres of forest
with an old steam engine,
pulling those stumps and plowing that sod,
to get five acres of scrub trees
on the shore of Devils Lake?
To haul that one car garage six miles
to this spot, to put in floor, windows,
and a chimney for a wood burning stove?

Was it worth planting
one of your acres in vegetables,
fishing for walleye and northern pike,
and getting meat from animals
that poached on your garden?
Did you can beans, corn, rabbit and venison
for the long, cold winters of North Dakota?
Did you emulate your seventy-five year old
papa's homesteading success in Saskatchewan?

This retreat let you live alone,
making other ends meet
by bartering your skills—
repairing clocks and radios
for coffee, flour, sugar, and salt.
Light work for a retired blacksmith
and machine shop owner,
but then this was the decade
of the Great Depression.

Acoma Pueblo

A mesa hovers hundreds of feet above
the saguaro cacti on the desert floor.
On top, dreamy Acoma Pueblo smokes
lore from mesquite fires in adobe stoves.
A shaman, smoldering embers like blood
at his feet, witnesses an ancient rite,
the blessing of the town.
Lines of the people pour powdery corn
on cloth and chant and chant.

To keep alive the sense of Pueblo—
the ground, the rock, the winds of the range
and all those that came and lived and died before—
a procession of souls circles the holy soil,
men of age recall The Pueblo Revolt
by firing rifle bullets at ghosts below.

Oxford, Mississippi

William Faulkner, born in Albany,
Mississippi, lived mostly
in Oxford, where he attended the University
briefly, then spent the rest of his life
writing novels and poetry there.

My wife and I, both educators who had not
visited any place in the southeastern
United States decided to travel to
New Orleans, Louisiana, to an American
Studies conference that I attended in 1972.

With an entire week off from our teaching duties,
we rented a car and made a side trip to Oxford.
There we visited the University of Mississippi
and Rowan Oak, an estate Faulkner
had purchased in his later years.
It took several days to get a good feel
for this part of the country.

After, we drove to Jackson, Mississippi to see
where author Eudora Welty had lived.
There we encountered a small village of
Black Americans living in a former
slave colony on stilted posts.
Shameful American history brought to life
before our eyes.

Dreamland Europe

I
My wife Helen and I, both educators, lived our dream
about visiting major countries and cities of Europe
of a two-month journey, beginning June 24, 1986.

We landed in Paris, took a train to our hotel near
Sylvia Beach's Shakespeare and Co. bookstore in the
French Quarter. Across the river Seine, we saw the
Notre Dame Cathedral, the Louvre, the Eiffel Tower,
the Tuileries, and experienced several centuries of
Dutch, Italian and French painters. We were
marveled by da Vinci's *Mona Lisa* up close.

We took photographs, made copious notes,
and discussed at all meals how these collections
would enhance teaching our students
back home in Bremerton, Washington.

We went on to locate the places where
Hemingway, Jack Kerouac, T.S. Eliot, Allen
Ginsburg and William Burroughs had stayed
when they visited Paris.
We even got to see Gertrude Stein's residence
where she and Toklas
hosted evenings for American artists.

One evening, we encountered an unexpected event
near our hotel—a large group of college-aged
individuals held a protest that brought out
a large fleet of police vans with numerous officers
surrounding several square blocks.
It brought to mind protests of similar-aged students
at the Haight-Ashbury in San Francisco during the 1960s.

II
At the start of the second week of our journey,
we picked up an Opel rental car for a two-week
sojourn beginning with Nice.

At the Chartres Cathedral we heard
a lecture by Malcolm Miller on the nature of this
Gothic cathedral, its 12th Century Architecture,
learned how the windows told a moral story
about God, love, and penance.

After the lecture, we walked the stone streets
of the old city, trees everywhere, and each home was
was surrounded by wall eight feet high.

Another day, we toured Amboise Chateaux
along the Loire river, the countryside there
similar to the upper plains of America.
These French raised crops such as corn, wheat,
and sunflower seeds.
The Loire itself reminded us of the Missouri river
except for acres and acres of grapes growing nearby
and houses built of stone or bricks with slate or tile roofs.

We also visited Chateaux of Blois, Chambord, and Claremont,
then drove to Bordeaux with its massive wine fields and wineries.

Next, we drove to Figures, Spain to visit the Salvador Dali
Museum, filled with Surreal, Cubist, and Impressionist art.
After several stops at hotels and shopping adventures
to get memoranda of our trip, we stopped in Arles, France
to see if we could get a sense of Van Gogh there.

The next day we left for Nimes to see a Roman Amphitheater.
Then onto to Avignon, the city of the Popes.
On the road once more, we stopped off in Antibes to see

the Musée Picasso. Finally, we made our way back to Nice
for a train to Rome the next day.

III
After a full day and night on the train,
we arrived in Rome, our hotel near the Spanish steps
where John Keats (one of my favorite poets) died.
We sat on the steps below where Keats had
a small pension room, imagining his time there.

After lunch, we visited the Vatican Museum with art
on display by Belvedere, Laocoon, Raphael and others.
After walking to St. Peter's Square, we entered the basilica
filled with paintings, ornate altars, the tomb of St. Peter,
the renowned *Pietà* statue by Michelangelo,
and of course, its dome, the tallest in the world.
Our senses over-awed, we returned to our hotel
for a siesta as the Italians do.
By nine we were off to dinner, a bit early for true natives.

In the days following, we visited the Coliseum, Forum,
Palatine, Pantheon, National Art Gallery, Palazzo Corsine,
Bernini's *David*, returned to the Vatican Museum,
and visited the Sistine Chapel with its halls filled with
sculpture, much by Romans of earlier times.
Last, we stopped at the American Academy,
where American artists lived and practiced their arts.
None of the American sites Helen and I had visited,
in such American cities as Chicago, New York,
Washington, D.C., and Boston, could compare
with Europe's statuary, huge artful buildings, and art by
artists from throughout the world.

Next, day we took a train to Florence, checked into our hotel
and walked a few streets before dining and sleeping.

After breakfast we rushed off to the Academy Gallery
to see Michelangelo's 18-foot high marble statue of David
and Botticelli's *Madonna*, also Michelangelo's unfinished *Pietá*.

The following day, we visited the Uffizi Gallery and saw paintings
by Paul Veronese, Botticelli, and Leonardo de Vinci.
Finally, we devoted a day to music by Berlioz and Tchaikovsky,
including *Symphonie Fantastique* and *Romeo and Juliet*.

IV
Leaving Rome, we rode a train to Venice, then sailed
the Grand Canal to our hotel.
Once checked in, we visited the Peggy Guggenheim Gallery
and the Academic Gallery, then walked among the islands
via bridges, stopping to dine al fresco along the way.
In the evening, we attended Venice's Latymer School
of London to hear Mozart and Vivaldi.

In the morning, we visited the Doge's Palace, then saw Paul Klee's
art in the Modern Art Gallery. Afterwards, we took a day-long
train ride to Vienna, Austria. That evening, we attended
a performance of Strauss's Waltz and opera music at the
Vienna Opera House. On Sunday, we strolled the Danube river to
Sigmund Freud's home and Museum.

Next day, we picked up a rental car and drove to Salzburg.
Two evenings, one of them our wedding anniversary,
gave us music by Mozart, Haydn, and Tchaikovsky.

Onto Germany the next day, the country of our ancestors,
Speyer and Rulzheim, where the Heckers had their beginnings
when Napoleon invaded and set up the Confederation of the
    Rhine.
George Hecker my great, great, great grandfather left Germany
    in 1809.

A few years after our trip, I would discover I had
relatives in Hamburg, but while there
we did meet a Hecker who was a Professor
at the University of Heidelberg who took us to visit a castle
with royal apartments, crumbling walls and moats
and also gave us a tour of the old university campus.

V
After nearly two months travel, my wife and I landed at Sea-Tac
Airport on August 15, 1986, went through security checks,
picked up our luggage, caught a shuttle bus to Seattle's
Colman Dock and boarded a ferry to our home in Bremerton.
I felt insecure.
Where were the ancient stone walls, foreigners, cathedrals
of long vintage, walled-in towns that had housed monarchs?
Where could I walk on stone streets a thousand years old?
Where were statues comparable to Bernini's *David*,
Michelangelo's *Pietà*?

Andalusia

While in Andalusia, stop at Granada
and visit the Alhambra—
its gardens and pools triggered
Washington Irving's imagination.

Stroll through Lorca's Memorial Garden,
a tribute to dance, deep song and bullfighting.
Row upon row of flowering shrubs circle his home,
remind you to lay bouquets in the Granada hills
where Franco's Army buried him.

Climb to the Albaicin Quarter,
near gypsy caves, and lunch on media barca.
Enter a luthier's shop below on a hillside
street and view acoustic guitars.
Be patient and stay, even though
you must decline the offer
to try out one of those rosewood
and spruce beauties,
for at any moment a guitarist will walk in
and pull one off the wall.

He will begin by running through scales,
chords, and arpeggios,
listening intently for just the right tone
and maybe a false vibration.
When he begins to play,
a tune by Albeniz,
maybe "Zambra Granadina,"
a woman whom you hadn't seen,
raises her arms and claps a set of castanets.

Slowly, as if rehearsed,
she swivels her body and clicks her heels

in rhythmic counterpoint
to the visceral bass notes of the guitar
and the luthier's staccato
clapping and high-pitched singing.

Before long, the three will take you
into a dream of mystery and spirit,
a place called *duende*.

Plaza de Bibarrambla

If you strolled a plaza in Granada,
next to a cathedral where women
offered sprigs from bushes,
then you witnessed an unusual procession,
a threesome that took your breath away.

These men stepped across the plaza in single file.
The first, tall and thin with shaggy,
shoulder-length hair, wore disheveled, dark clothing.
He lurched forward, intent on a destination,
carried a sack full of corked bottles.

The second man in a frayed muscle shirt,
wore leather vest and jeans, modeled blonde,
stringy, shoulder-length hair.
His heavily muscled arms and shoulders strained
against the strides of a mastiff on a leash.

The third man bounced along,
doing pirouettes
Taller than the other two, and shirtless, his dark,
wrinkled, open full-length overcoat,
revealed a chest of long, curly black hair.

In the middle of the plaza, with arms raised,
face lifted and tongue extended, he whirled
in circles, as if attacking a toreador's cape,
hissed and snorted at the sky,
then bowed and quickly and disappeared
from the plaza just past the Moorish bazaar.

Antiquity Now

Bumping our luggage by lively
tavernas and shops, my wife and I
walk the cobbled streets
of the Plaka section of Athens,
following a young Greek woman,
a good Samaritan, we met
on a tram from the airport.

After settling in our hotel, we stroll
down an alley and look up at
the objective of our journey,
The Acropolis.

On an earlier trip to London,
we marveled at the Elgin Marbles
on display in the British Museum,
looted and hauled there by Lord Elgin
in the first years of 1800.
These exquisite sculptures motivated us
to dream of and travel to the Parthenon.

We had been treated well by people
on the streets, giving us directions,
suggesting sights we had not seen
and finally by giving us the name
of a special restaurant
in the Plaka area, near our hotel,
that had red wine, Greek salad,
baked zucchini, and grilled pork.

At the late hour we returned
to our hotel, told the concierge,
a middle-aged Austrian,
about our contacts with Greeks,

including the good Samaritan.
She said she enjoyed Athens
because the people are human.
She discovered this on vacations
and believed they had this quality
in their genes, inherited from the
early Greek city-states when humanity
was deeply prized and passed on.
Those city-states are an example
of antiquity now.

The next morning, we entered
the Theatre of Dionysus
to take photos and absorb the thrill
of imagining what it was like
to attend a play here in ancient times.

Relaxed and ready, we ventured up
to the entrance of the Temple of Athena.
The ticket attendant laughed,
said that Zeus was the unfaithful God
but the royalty of all the Gods.
Her humor was typical of
the friendly humanness
of the Greek people we met.

In perfect weather,
we witnessed the Acropolis,
the Erechtheum, and the Parthenon.
We reveled in their beauty in spite of
cracked columns and worn marble.
We sat on broken stones, absorbing the moment.

The next morning we rushed to catch our home
for the next ten days: *The Jade*, a cruise ship
that would take us to more of our dreams of
antiquity, including Olympia, Alexandria, and Istanbul.

Whirling Dervishes

I sit in the audience reading a handout
that describes a dance of Istanbul,
a form of meditation for the Islamic
sect of Sufism.
Since I meditate in a Buddhist Sangha
in my hometown,
I look forward to this spiritual ceremony.

Five men dressed in black play
drums, string instruments.
One sings in a piercing tone.
High pitched rhythmic notes fill the room.

Four other men enter, clad in black robes,
foot-high white cone-shaped hats.
They throw their robes
between the seated musicians,
revealing white shirts, high-collared
white tunic jackets and floor length
skirts with black cummerbunds.

Stepping to the corners of the dance floor,
they face each other and start whirling in place.
As they turn, the skirts lift and blossom.
Spinning rapidly for five minutes,
with eyes closed and heads cocked,
the dancers wear rapt facial expressions.

I feel intense and ecstatic, full of joy,
as when I witnessed Sioux and Blackfeet tribes
of the Great Plains performing a dance with music
and fire, a Sun Dance to honor the sun and
bring world renewal and thanksgiving.

I leave the hall rejuvenated
and walk the street towards Hagia Sophia,
once a Christian church,
then an Islamic mosque, now a museum.
A few women pass in their burkas.
Old men thumb worry beads.
I instinctively reach to my right
pants pocket, but there is no rosary now.

Qin Shi Huang

Buried in formation
for thousands of years
until a farmer dug a well,
terra-cotta soldiers
stood captured in the moment.

Chariots, drivers and horses
remained at attention.

The models for these clay figures
carried on after the Emperor died,
surrogates to protect him
in the world beyond.

Three Gorges Dam

The cruise ship's twin props churn
the waters of the river,
carrying tourists from Chongqing
towards Shanghai.
The vessel cuts through smog,
by villages and farms
barely visible on riverbanks.

In a few months all will drown,
as the Three Gorges Dam
slowly backs up the Yangtze River.

The cruise ship docks,
releasing passengers to bargain
for remnants of local arts and crafts,
as workers dismantle the village.

Snuff bottles of clear crystal hold
interior paintings of swarming red, yellow,
blue butterflies and hummingbirds.

Wood block broadsides salute pastoral
settings of garden, orchard, folk.

Rabbit, horse and dragon top stone chops,
carry official seal, permit, name.

Youth of the village board a ferry,
departing for jobs in factories
near seaside ports.
Elders touch their creations
with fingers lingering,
then wave goodbye.
They will dream of their futures.

Crop rotation continues this last time.
Rice in ancient seedbeds sprouted in February
are replanted to fields and flooded by May.

By August, farmers sack the rice,
seed the dry paddy with
vegetables or winter wheat.

Water buffalo strain to till soil
for crops of squash,
mushrooms, tomatoes, bell peppers,
pumpkins and potatoes.

Pigs and chickens root and peck
in tangerine orchards.

Tugs, struggling upstream,
push coal barges to Chongqing.

Freighters, carrying new cars,
steam towards Shanghai.

A lonely sampan,
fishing lines slack, passes.

Chinese Busker in Shanghai

Dressed in a faded blue Mao suit,
and wearing green tennis shoes,
an old man sits on a wooden stool,
playing an erhu.
He's blind.

He sings softly as his dark hair washes
across his blank eyes,
and his face stiffens
to our approaching English words.

Does he sing of Lao-Tzu and the Way,
of Chou, Han, and Tang dynasties,
of Mao's Long March
and the Cultural Revolution,
of Tiananmen Square in 1987,
of Economic Free Zones?

The busker's worn cap
lies on the concrete.
Crumpled paper Yuan
and coins nest in it.
I add a crisp dollar bill.
Does he sense the weight
of American money?

La Chascona, Neruda's Home

What is a home to you?
Is it a place to raise a family?
To some it's just a shelter.
To many it's an investment.
To a few it's a display of wealth.
To me it's where I live
with my wife and write.

Pablo Neruda dreamed La Chascona
as a way to express his flair for design,
and to display his large collections,
to write, to live with his mistress,
and to entertain guests.

La Chascona, meaning wild mane of hair,
was named after Pablo's nickname for Matilda.

The home began as a shack
Neruda purchased at the bottom of
San Christobal Hill in Santiago.
The land included forest with scrubs
and berry plants up the sloope
to the top of the hill.

Outside the entrance,
a terrace with stone enclosures,
and a garden of jasmines, camellias,
copihues, and roses.
Along one side of the exit door,
a painting of a fried fish on a copihue—
Chile's national flower—
and birds painted around the door
and to the right of it.

Pablo and Matilda enjoyed transforming
the shack, furnishing the rooms to capture
his collections of doorknobs, door knockers,
agates, figureheads, shells, statues, glasses,
metal cups, wine glasses and dishware,
all collected during his time as a diplomat
in Burma, Argentina, Mexico, Spain, and France

The rooms above the remodeled shack
connected to other rooms up the slope
with stone stairs and metal railings
that resembled ocean waves.

Pablo hired masons and carpenters
to build the structures,
and designers to build
doors with glass windows
and metal figures.
Artists created framed paintings
and painted marine oil figures on walls.

The top room of the home,
a studio with bar where Pablo
wrote poems and entertained guests,
displayed a framed portrait of
Walt Whitman on a stone wall.
A carpenter who framed the portrait
asked Pablo if it was his father.
Pablo answered,
"Yes, it is my father...in poetry."

Pablo said that if he hadn't become a poet,
he would have been a builder.
With La Chascona, Pablo was both builder
and poet, for he designed the rooms just like
he would edit and revise a poem,

adding images, themes, and rhythms.
The sections of the home
were like stanzas of a poem.

Literary Day in Dublin

I stroll along the quays
bordering the Liffey
until I arrive at Trinity,
the location of the *Book of Kells*.

I marvel at its calligraphy, symbols,
and illustrations in blue,
green and black-brown ink
on cream-colored sheep vellum.

Outside, the monks in their graves
feed the lawn and old, healthy maple trees.
The only headstone is a sculpture
by Henry Moore.

Up the street and around a corner,
I join a crowd of tourists
taking selfies with a life-size statue
of Molly Malone,
a character from Joyce's *Ulysses*.
She stands in dress and blouse,
holding the arms of a wheelbarrow
of cockles & mussels,
not the arms of Leopold Bloom.

As I stroll over a bridge towards
the Abbey Theatre,
an old man gives me directions
and warns me about pickpockets.
Is he a reincarnation of Bloom?

In the theater, I sit where plays
by Yeats were performed.
I was lucky to see "Donegal,"

a matinee musical, describing the Irish.
"They are a rough and tumble lot,"
says the grandma of the family.

Continuing up O'Connell,
I find the monument to Parnell
in an intersection.
I recall the Irish revolution against
British rule, and remember Yeats's poem
about Parnell's funeral:
> *Through Jonathan Swift's dark /*
> *grove he passed, //*
> *and there plucked bitter wisdom /*
> *that enriched his blood.*

Further up the street,
at the Dublin Writers' Museum
I encounter first edition books
written by Swift, Yeats,
Joyce, Beckett, Wilde, and Shaw.
Quotes from favored writings
by these authors hang on walls.
Shaw's captured my attention:
> *You use a mirror to see your face;*
> *you use works of art to see your soul.*

Notes, inscriptions, portraits of these writers
are featured in many rooms of the house,
reminding me of characters and scenes
in books and plays by Beckett.

Two blocks away,
at the James Joyce Cultural Center,
I take a selfie in front of
a haunting, life-sized portrait of Joyce.
I label it *two poets commiserate.*

Other photos of Joyce and his wife Nora
decorate the walls along with quotes
from *Ulysses* and *Dubliners*
on a computer screen.
I follow Leopold Bloom
in parts of his day-long trek of
Dublin and see a film of "The Dead,"
one of the stories in *Dubliners*.

Later, one the other side of Dublin,
at the Temple Bar area,
music from the pubs fill the streets.
I enter one, enjoy a pint of Guinness,
and listen to two guitar players singing
Irish songs and popular foreign tunes.
I order Irish stew, soda bread,
and a glass of Jameson to complete
my Irish literary day with a full stomach
as well as a full soul.

Departure in 1893

I
Thorbjorg turns and looks back
at her fishing village—
birth place and home for seventeen years.
Small wood frame houses stand near the water,
huddle together like a flock of seabirds
in cold, gray mists.
A few bluewater fishing boats
are anchored in the fjord.
Rowboats rest upon the shore.
A famine has descended on the Island,
reducing population like winter storms at sea
during fishing season.

Her parents, Thorvald and Lara,
will live in this village
until they rest above
on a shelf of land, the Holy Ground.

Thorbjorg will not miss her father's
drinking bouts after arctic fishing voyages.
She will not miss filleting cod,
hanging them on high racks to dry,
or butchering whales on the beach.
She will not miss the dark, rainy weather
or the treeless volcanic soil.

II
Thorbjorg steps on up a wagon trail,
carrying a bag on her shoulder
stuffed with clothes, healer herbs, dried codfish,
Bible, a few kronur, and passage papers
on a ship sailing to Canada.

As she plods along at a funeral's pace,
a ptarmigan flies from a boggy meadow
of cotton grass, buttercups and dandelions.
She pauses and wonders if she will see
this type of bird in the new place,
hear the cooing of a golden plover
or the warbling trill of a whimbrel
She will dream that she will.

III

Her ship sails out of Akureyri in six days.
Thorbjorg picks up her pace, for it will take
four days or more to walk to that port city.
She climbs out of the fjord past rugged, rock walls.
Caves remind her of the Hidden People
who are known to help travelers.

Thorbjorg plans to rest in tiny, empty churches
to read Psalms and snack on dried fish.
She will stop in the evenings
at crofts for bed and board.
She knows she must continue
her journey across the ocean to Canada
to start afresh in an Icelandic community
in Saskatchewan.
Each night of her journey she will
dream of a new beginning,
of creating her new life.

Havamals for Traveling Iceland's Circle

1
Drive a car
or catch a bus.
Tour Iceland's Circle.

See Peaks, waterfalls,
sheep and puffins.
Park and snap photos.

2
Survey horse
and sheep pastures.
Peer at croft houses.

Stare at glaciers,
single lane steel bridges.
Be ready to stop.

3
Pause to picnic.
Breathe pure air.
You won't need pollen pills.

Dip water at streams
from snow on ridges.
Drink, enjoy hydration.

4
Turf house remains
on fjord roadways
are more than relics.

Craftsmen lost sheep.
Children froze.
Courts ended love affairs.

5
Vikings left myths
above a lava butte,
a place of legend.

Visitors hike it.
Will they be hailed
by elves or hidden people?

6
Cairns provided direction
for crofters in distant winters,
delivering goods to villages.

Roads parallel these markers,
provide insight to travelers.
Remind them that times change.

7
Rugged rock ridges
like pyramids in a row
rise on the horizon.

Cloud covered
narrow roads
require stops for passage.

8
Steam and hot water
spray from geothermal pools
beneath the surface.

Hot water pumped
to towns provides
heat for houses and showers.

II Dangers

You hold the world in your hand
as if it were a cold bright bead...
But what about my boy,
Did you enjoy his taste?
—Anna Akhmatova

Whatever you
Can do, or dream
You can, begin
It.
—Johan Wolfgang von Goethe

Armed Forces Day Parade, 2004

In late morning, viewers gather
on both sides of Main Street.
They crowd together six feet deep
with the front line sitting
on the curb or lawn chairs.
Some have coolers with snacks and drinks.
Many wave flags.

A veteran, newly discharged from Iraq War,
leans on his crutches, one leg gone.
His wife holds a newborn to her breast.
Sunglasses shield her eyes but not her tears.
She gazes at her child wrapped
in an old towel, her husband's face.

A wave of cheers washes over the crowd
as late model, shiny convertibles round
the corner, weave through potholed streets,
carrying the Captain
of the local naval command,
heads of veterans' groups.
and Miss Hometown Queen.

A military band follows,
led by high school baton twirlers.
The band members, marching in unison,
lean, straight limbed,
belt out the notes of
"The Star-Spangled Banner."

The drummers beat louder
as the band passes,
and the crowd heaves, pushing

the young mother and child forward.
Mom trips on the cracked curb,
and they tumble.

The husband lunges to break their fall,
collapses on top of them in a heap.
The clamor is so frenzied
that no one notices
as the ex-soldier and family
struggle to get to their feet.

658

We ferry passengers watch
two tugs guide a sperm whale
heading home through Rich Passage.

The somnolent whale sprays vapor
out its blowhole and doesn't
seem to mind our passing.

Pressed against the rail,
we peer at the lethal mammal,
knowing its potential.

We search for its name.
We whisper to each other.
Secretly we fear it.

The whale's pilot fish work along
its back, swabbing attentively.
Sonar pulses measure our hull.

Slowly the whale moves to berth,
floats along breathless,
to rest a spell before sinking.

Hitchhiking

The only time I ever hitchhiked,
my thumb attracted the driver
of a sixteen-wheeler.
He said he needed company
to stay awake,
been on the road for eighteen hours,
hauling a huge caterpillar
on the back of his rig.

I was headed to my hometown
a hundred miles away
to visit friends,
cruise familiar streets,
and dance to rock and roll.

Nodding his head for me to climb in,
he reached second gear,
then slumped forward
onto the steering wheel.

I shook his shoulder fiercely.
He woke, stopped the truck, asked,
"Do you know how to drive?"
I said I'd driven grain trucks on farms.
We exchanged places, and he told me
to double clutch between forward gears,
then fell asleep again.

When I reached forty miles per hour,
the road looked narrow
like a path on the prairies,
and the speed seemed like sixty.

The first town I entered,
and the only one I would pass through
with a stop light,
I tried to slow,
but I didn't think to double clutch
down through the gears.
Thank goodness it was dinnertime
and few drivers were on the main street.

The next stop was my former hometown.
I managed to halt the truck on the outskirts.
The driver awakened and thanked me.
I was still shaking as I climbed out
of the truck and stepped down
onto the safety of solid ground.

Rescue

On a day climb, we hike
up a trail through cedar and fir.
Mount Ellinor towers
above us with snow fields,
ridges and peak.

We navigate scree in chutes
like salmon struggling over rapids.
We rope up, crunch along
with step and rest,
step and rest,
up snow slopes and past crevasses
until we reach the summit.
We sit, admire Hood Canal below.

The way down offers respite,
for we glissade,
un-roped with day packs
on our backs, ice axes as rudders,
sliding down slopes
on boots and behinds.

As we reach the last snowfield,
one climber tops a slight mound
and slips one foot into a small crevasse.
He breaks an ankle.

One of our mountain rescue leaders
secures the climber's ankle with
cut saplings and crafts a carrier
out of tree limbs and rope.

We other climbers carry,
alternate side-to-side,

one hand on the load,
the other on an ice axe.

Hearing water running below
the snowfield, we decide
to secure our injured man by
belaying him from behind
The final rescue is
a car ride to the urgent care.

Dangers on the Slopes

We quit removing our crampons
when someone yells, "Listen!"
We hear *skip, skip, skip.*
Everyone looks up the slope.
A twenty-pound rock is leaping
down at us.

One of our leaders, sitting alone
in the center of the chute, stands,
turns, judges the rock's angle of flight,
and leans his body away.
The stone plunges by his head.

I hear a few "luck's with us."
We're all shaken, but start to glissade
with ice axes as rudders.
I say "What a disaster after a summit climb."
My partner answers, "We're lucky
it wasn't an avalanche!"

Our rope team, the last to cross
Nisqually Glacier above a huge crevasse,
reach the halfway point
when my partner shouts, "Falling!"

I dive onto the slope, plunge
my ice axe blade into the snow's crust,
dig my crampon-fitted boots into the ice.
His weight drags me a foot,
ripping ice and snow into my face.
I'm sweating, fearing I won't
see my wife and two children again.

After what seems like an hour,
I turn my head slowly and see my partner
laying spread eagle just feet
from the gaping crevasse.
He shouts he's OK and has his ice axe.
I belay him as he steps up the slope.

We continue, carefully using kick steps,
reach safety at our base camp,
my last one on any mountain.

Marriage Road

We've travelled the road
of marriage for fifty years
with quite a few bumps
along the way.

Sometimes the road was gravel,
sometimes pavement,
and at other times, like
the autobahn carrying us at
high speeds into the unknown.

Now in our seventies,
we no longer travel any road.
We walk in public parks and
along suburban sidewalks
rarely encountering
bumps in our travels.

We do dream about the old days
of zooming along,
but we put those dreams aside
as no longer applicable to our lives.

Dream or Reality

The dog, dead for years, keeps
coming back in a dream. We look
at each other with the old joy. It was
always her gift to bring me back into the present—
　　　　　—Jane Hirshfield

Coming out of anesthesia was like
waking up from a dream
during a deep sleep
but not remembering anything.
Maybe my muse,
who enters my dreams
with hints to improve a poem
I had in process,
didn't want me to remember my surgery.

Others experience loss of memory from
amnesia, concussion, auto accidents, and stroke.
A friend flew to Amsterdam,
bought hashish and sat on a bench
near the Anne Frank Museum.
He chewed hashish and woke two hours later
two miles across the city,
not remembering how he got there
and what he had done along the way.

I was checked into surgery for
an anterior total left hip replacement.
I lay on a roller bed in a gown.
A surgical assistant placed an IV
connection into my right arm.
Another assistant inserted a needle
into my spine, injecting me with anesthesia.

What happened after the injection?

I didn't notice being rolled to the surgery room.
I didn't feel the IV bag getting hooked up.
I didn't feel the insertion of the urinary catheter
into my penis.
I didn't feel the four-inch scalpel
cut into my upper left thigh and hip.
I didn't feel the surgeons move my thigh muscles
to the sides of my upper femur bone.
I didn't feel the removal of my upper femur
bone and ball.
I didn't feel my surgeon cutting osteoarthritic spurs
from around my pelvic cup area.
I didn't feel pain or see masked, gloved surgeons.
I didn't feel the placement of a new pelvic cup.
I didn't feel the insertion of a new upper
portion of femur bone and new ball
into my old femur bone.

I didn't feel the placement of the new
femur addition and ball into my new pelvic cup.
I didn't feel pain at the repositioning
of my thigh muscles and
the suturing of the four-inch cut.

Weeks have passed,
and my muse hasn't entered
my dreams about this exploration
of hip surgery and anesthesia,
likely because I experienced a real event
with factual results, not a new poem.

Precarious Waterfront

From the deck of a ferryboat,
not long after 9/11,
gleaming glass buildings—
the Black Box, a Dutch barn roof—
two towers just under the airport route
to Sea-Tac International Airport.

Commuters race their cars
along the sinking Alaska Way Viaduct,
a target for future earthquakes.

In the distance,
Mt. Rainier's west facing flank
shines an icy white glow
with rocky ribs jutting downwards.
The mountain's summit is obscured
in powdery, wind-driven clouds.
Steam rises out of its peak
from molten lava deep inside
this hot volcano.

A U.S. Coast Guard boat,
displays a high caliber cannon on its bow,
patrols beside another ferry.
A bulging freight ship slides past.

Port facility cranes
frame the twin domes
of Quest and Safeco Fields.
Container vessels moor along the wharves,
waiting to unload their cargos,
including hidden refugees from Asian shores.

Our ferry docked, vehicles drive off
onto streets, passengers hurry along
elevated walkways.
Below, state highway patrolmen
and dogs hunt for explosives
in the rows of cars waiting to board.

Vision

A philosopher once wrote,
"The world is my representation."
We may not know precisely
what he meant,
but each of us possess
a unique world without
really being conscious of it.

We don't see what is actually
in the world before us.

What we see is a representation
of the thing we think we see.
What we see is a reflection
on the iris of our eyes that is
filtered through memories.

What we have learned
about aspects of objects
from family, religion, nation,
and education reflects what we see.

A color, a word that represents
that color, releases an emotion,
desire, thought or bias.
What we see is
an accumulation of many responses
but never the thing itself.

Squirrels

During this Covid-19 Era of vaccinations and masks,
many of us hibernate in our homes, avoiding exposure
at theatres, sports arenas, museums, shopping malls.
Books, hobbies, arts, and correspondence with family and
friends help prevent disease and boredom, while Zoom,
television, and music keep us from crashing into depression.

This winter, nature offers another pastime, watching
squirrels in the park next to our condo building.
Grey squirrels make caves in the red oak and chestnut trees,
burrow under rhododendrons alongside the park's pathways.
When the trees shed their leaves, squirrels dig into the piles
to harvest acorns, hickory nuts, maple seeds, berries, mushrooms,
and the leaves themselves for nests in trees and burrows.

Another marvel is how the squirrels scramble after each other,
from one section of the leaves to another.
At times, squirrels scamper after each other up the larger oak trees
to large limbs and out onto branches that are thinner—
frightening to watch because as they jump from one small branch
to another, they nearly fall twenty feet to the ground below.

Barred Owl

The Owl's claws lock deep in the
rabbit's fur, and the owl seated
a little sideways, his mind on something else;
the rabbit's ears are back, his eyes intent.
...But the dream has never got any further.
　　　　　—Elizabeth Bishop

Sometime in July or August
just before sunrise,
hike up a hillside
amid fir and cedar trees.
Look for the Barred Owl.

Bring your camera,
for if you're lucky
you'll see one
high up a tall tree.

To spot the owl,
look for large dark eyes
starring at you from a face
circled with a brown strip
above a chest of dark brown streaks
on a lighter brown coat.

The owl might warn you
with a *hoo-hoo, hoo-ah*
since it's breeding season.
Beware, for the Barred Owl
might swoop down and snatch
your cap or hat,
you being an intruder.

Territory

A ring-necked rooster pheasant,
brilliant in red, brown and blue plumage,
patrols a field of dense grass and brush,
chortling his territorial rights.

A coyote, hearing the cock's call,
enters the wild grass and dense brush.
The rooster rockets to a red oak limb,
squawking and bringing attention to itself.
The coyote bounces about the field,
invites the rooster to play.

The rooster continues to call out to the coyote.
The coyote tires, stretches out on the grass,
but his ears prick, and he peers into the brush,
enters, and in a minute returns with a
mottled brown corpse in his mouth.
The coyote carries it away, causing
the rooster to shriek wildly.

The rooster dives down into the grass,
enters the brush with no chortling.
A month later a young ring-necked rooster
flies away with the larger male pheasant.

Spider and Gnat

From my deck, I admire
a blossoming horse chestnut.
White and pink flowers feed
honeybees and hummingbirds.
Chestnuts drop from stems
for squirrels.

I'm reading Ursula K. Le Guin's
latest poetry book, *Late in the Day*.
One poem marks time passing—
"in times womb begins all ending."

Inside the deck railing,
a spider grapples with a gnat
caught in its web.
The spider circles around and
up and down spinning,
encasing its struggling prey.

Camera and magnifying glass
capture the battle,
and a baby spider
waits like a chick in a nest.

The gnat quits, enmeshed.
The large spider remains still,
hanging an inch from the gnat,
as though exhausted.

But soon the spider moves under
the gnat, pushing its head up,
sucking fluids out.

Le Guin's words define nature—
"While kind and unforgiving Earth
Endures our brief disaster."

Revolutions

Revolutions seem distant
when we read about them.
Even photographs hold us
but temporarily, like words
from the evening news.

But discover that one
of your kinsmen was shot
beside his home in 1917
because of mistaken identity,
then, then revolutions mean.

Tour Guide at Ushuaia

When you arrive at Ushuaia,
the southernmost seaport
in Argentina, think of Magellan's
first circumnavigation of the globe
around Cape Horn.
Look forward to viewing
his statue in Punta Arenas.

Take a three-day cruise
and climb to the top of Cape Horn
in fierce winds on a clear day,
snap selfies of the Horn's Monument
and gaze at the South Pole.
Rush when your guide says you must
hurry down to rubber rafts
to get to the cruise ship or be stranded.

The ship motors into an area of
1200 glaciers in fjords at the southern rim
of Tierra Del Fuego.
Dressed in heavy clothing
and safety vests aboard a rubber raft,
your guide warns you about
the changing climate that is causing
the glaciers to recede.

The last stop on the cruise is
a penguin colony on the shore of an island.
It is mating season and male penguins
prepare nests for females to lay their eggs.
The males haul seaweed across the path

but wait for you to pass.
You photograph these courteous creatures,
while your guide informs that theft
of seaweed is constant.

After you return to Ushuaia,
your guide recounts his past life
in the surrounding hills and mountains.
He can identify all edible plants,
berries and roots, he can fish, hunt,
and start a fire without matches.
He asks, "What are you going to do
when the lights go out?"

III Voices

Those who dream by day are cognizant of many
things which escape those who dream only by night.
—Edgar Allan Poe

All that I am hangs by a thread tonight
as I wait for her whom no one can command.
Whatever I cherish most—youth freedom
glory—
fades before her who bears the flute in her hand.
—Anna Akhmatova

My Sister Veronica

I stop at your grave,
a granite stone just level
with the cut grass,
place an orange rose
in your flower vase.

Remember picnics at Cheyenne River
with our vast and curious clan.
Some of our uncles wore bib-overalls,
denim shirts and straw hats. They stuck
bamboo fishing pools into the riverbank,
watched red and white bobbers for nibbles or strikes.
Our dad stood with rod and reel, casting daredevils.
Our mom and aunts commandeered ice chests,
picnic baskets, and blankets while gossiping
about absent relatives and their ailments.

We cousins plunged into the murky water,
doing cannonballs and belly flops.
Swimming and diving below the surface,
we bumped into bullheads and perch.
Devouring hotdogs, potato salad, and Kool-Aid,
we lounged on sweet prairie grass,
breathed air filled with scents of cut hay
and maturing clover crop,
listened to twittering meadowlarks.

Afternoons, we played tag, softball and flew kites
until we dropped back into the water to cool off.
If our dad and uncles caught enough fish,
we lingered into evening amid mosquitoes and wasps,
ate fried fish and potatoes with fresh vegetables,
and sucked down more Kool-Aid.

Remember the rides home in our old Chevy—
two parents with six kids on top of each other
like calves in a trailer on the way to market.

Dear sweet, Veronica,
born June 1, 1937,
died June 1, 1937,
you don't remember any of it
but I still dream of you being there.

Way of Life or Love?

Two roads diverged in a wood, and I—
I took the one less traveled by,
and that has made all the difference.
—Robert Frost

Down the hillside,
near the swirling waters
of a rising tide,
Eli lights a fire by his workshop.
He burns chunks of wood and shavings
from cedar planks and oak beams.
As he warms his hands,
he looks up at his empty cottage.

His wife Elna wants a car,
but he already has
a small rowboat with outboard motor.
Grocery store, Sears and Roebuck,
clinic, and post office were all
within walking distance of a public dock
where they could tie up.

Eli looks up and smiles
at his double-ended, half-finished hull,
a thirty-two-foot ketch.
He rubs his hand down one oak rib,
turns and lifts a beam
onto a set of sawhorses,
looks at pencil marks,
reaches for a long blade saw.

Sandra's Vow

She drives out
of the parking lot.
Moist air, rising breeze
and dark clouds—
a change in weather.

She taxies the streets
towards the freeway.
Rain taps the roof.
Wipers stroke
the splattered windshield.

Will Bill remember
to get Sue after piano?
What to do for dinner?
Pick up Pizza Hut takeout.
She taps its number, waits, orders
a large pepperoni and sausage.

Headlights illuminate
water standing in dips.
Rivulets flow into storm sewers.
Pedestrians pull coats tighter,
lower umbrellas into the wind.

Sandra's cell phone rings.
Her supervisor's name
appears on the screen.
I'm not returning to the office now!
she shouts to herself.

On the freeway, Sandra
winces, grips the steering wheel,
peers through sheets of gusting rain,

accelerates, switches the wipers
to rapid speed.
Lightning flashes across the sky
reveals rolling,
charcoal clouds crashing
like breakers on a seashore.
Visibility drops to zero
as trucks speed by,
spraying waves of water
onto the car's windshield.

It's like she's in a carwash!
Her right front tire
hits a sea of standing water,
pulls the car towards the shoulder.
Swinging the wheel to the left
then quickly to the right,
she keeps the car from the adjoining lane.
Rain tattoos the roof.

An exit sign causes her to slow.
She rounds a curve
to an intersection,
stops at a red flickering light
that arcs overhead.
On green she crosses the roadway
into the Pizza Hut parking lot,
shuts off the engine,
screams at the windshield,
This is it! No more
God damned commuting!

Solo Guitarist

At a concert on Capitol Hill, Irina Kulikona,
a Russian classical guitarist,
played several selections, including
Claude DeBussy's "Clair de Lune"
and Augustin Barrios's "La Catedral."

When she announced "La Catedral"
I closed my eyes to listen with my whole
body to my favorite tune by Barrios,
hoping it would be like gazing at a full moon
in a clear night sky.

Irina played superbly, using the fingerstyle
method with no strumming.
The audience clapped and I yelled "Bravo."

Irina got up from her chair and bowed,
looking down at her guitar,
a gift from a master guitarist
when she was eight years old,
nearly in tears.

Music charms us into bliss just as dreams do.

Denise Levertov

A transplant first from England,
then from the East Coast
to Seattle's Seward Park area,
Denise lived near herons
in view of Mt. Rainier.

A civilian nurse during World War II,
after the war ended, she married
and moved to New York city,
became an American citizen by 1955.

I met her first by phone.
She drove a hard bargain to give
a keynote address at my college's
annual writers' conference.

She was worth it,
not just for her speech and presence,
but also for the long conversation
we had about our family histories.
We both laughed when I told her
I was a "retired" Catholic,
a faith she had just joined.

Her funeral wasn't
the last time I saw Denise.
In Seward Park, where I sat
on a bench and gazed at lily pads
and other dense foliage, I caught
sight of a heron on a post in the water.

The bird squawked
then hopped to another post
directly in front of me.

I can't explain why but I immediately
thought it was Denise
and drifted into memories
of our long conversation.

When I looked up again,
the heron was gone.
I had missed its flight, but I would dream
often about this encounter.

Iambs for the New Age

Each day I enter e-mail
to sort the store of trash and gold.
Trash is stuff about cafe entrees,
about unclaimed items,
about unneeded meetings, jokes,
and dates for blood donations.
Corrections, sayings, cancellations.
Stop! Delete!

The gold lingers, awaiting response.
The least goes first, unless
special notes ignite the eye:
invites to call, to meet, to golf,
to lunch, to rendezvous.
Decision time, compose, print, send
obligatory meetings next—
enter into index and store again, again.
A sparring match in bytes too, dejà vu.

The First Thread in Neruda's Life

Pablo Neruda was two months old
when his mother died.
This loss of love, warmth,
and nurturing must have led him to a life
pursuing that omission.

Substitutes in his youth were the Andes, forests,
and the Pacific shores near his birthplace
in Parral, Chile.

Gabriela Mistral, the headmistress
of his hometown school
introduced him to poets like Baudelaire,
Rimbaud, and Verlaine.

Teen-aged Pablo, inspired by these masters,
wrote his own verse and began pursing
his first love, Teresa, who was not
equally as smitten.

But Gabriela mentored Pablo into
a scholarship at a college in Santiago.
So at seventeen, he went off to the big city
wearing a black suit, wide-brimmed hat,
gray cape, ready to conquer the world.

Neruda spent his time reading
and writing poems during the day,
courting women and prowling bars
with fellow writers at night,
singing in French, English, and German.

By age nineteen, he lost his scholarship
and his allowance from his father.
He sold his watch, black suit, and furniture
to self-publish *Crepusculano*,
a forty-eight page collection of poems
no one seemed to notice.

But at age twenty, Neruda found his way
like an eagle landing in its nest,
a bird he thought he might return as,
if reincarnation was real.
His second collection,
Twenty Love Poems
was published and widely read
in Chile and other parts of Latin America.

The poems captured his love and thirst
for the women in images of nature.
The last poem in the collection
mourned how love was always
lost in the end.

Neruda would marry and divorce twice,
continue to have many mistresses,
But perhaps only Matilda,
his third wife,
came close to filling the emptiness
his mother's death left in his soul.

Never Give Up

Hermann Hesse died in his sleep
at age eighty-five
after listening to a Mozart sonata.
Such a slow, rhythmic beat must have
made him feel bliss,
as he flew into eternity forever.

He began his life in a labyrinth,
circling around and around,
without finding his way.
From age four, his parents fashioned his life
to make him a Protestant missionary.

First, he was housed and taught by a pastor,
except for church on Sundays when he saw his parents.
The lack of love and family made him think
he was an orphan.

Next, he was sent off to a missionary academy
to force him to become an advocate
of his parents' view of the world.

Hesse rebelled, left school, and ran away.
When he was caught and returned,
he attempted suicide.
For that, he was shipped off to an insane asylum,
then another, then tries at different professions,
including a mechanic apprenticeship
at a clock factory, the monotony of which
drove him to more spiritual pursuits.

Finally, an apprenticeship in a Tubingen, Germany bookstore began his journey to discover his voice, live his dream of being a writer.

Hermann Hesse never gave up on himself.

Time Off

Why ask me to stay when I want to stray?
My work is done, and I want to play in the sun.
It's just that way; let's call it a day.

The system, you say, will have its way.
But I don't fear a dun; I'm out for fun.
Why ask me to stay when I want to stray?

The work ethic, you say, will begin to fray.
A Puritan Past, I pun, can be overdone.
It's just that way; let's call it a day.

Think of commerce, you say, and how it pays.
I'll live to see, I plea, the sun set in homespun.
Why ask me to stay when I want to stray?

Orders we can't shun, you say, bills must be spun.
If today is done, I assert, they'll get none.
It's just that way; let's call it a day.

It's your civic duty, you say, as native son.
That kind of sham, I groan, I'll always shun.
Why ask me to stay when I want to stray?
It's just that way; let's call it a day.

Key West, Florida

January 1993

Over a half-century ago in Key West,
where Elizabeth Bishop, in exile, wrote poems,
letters and practiced "One Art,"
you strolled down Duval Street under palm
and mangrove trees,
floating on the scent of jasmine.

After dining on green turtle consommé,
oysters, rice, and mangoes,
you spent the evening at Sloppy Joe's rumba night.

You reveled in wood carving and flower folk art
observed convicts at large during the day,
locked-out at night,
and told stories about fortune tellers.

You preferred the side lanes
where locals ate conch fritters and callaloo,
cafes that welcomed poets.

Before dawn, you step onto Duval Street once again.
The full moon shines like a stage work light.
The only sounds: a cat's cry, a rooster's crow.

Balconies hang over storefronts
that shelter bikinis and Havana hats.

A woman of the night makes
a call at a pay phone:
catfish and hushpuppies, thirteen-fifty.

Wahoo and Amberjack hang
on Uncle Louie's back wall.
Soon he'll serve Cuban coffee at the counter.

In Memory of William Stafford

Oregonians feel the earth shudder.

Ducks stray from their flight paths.

Salmon pause in their upstream struggle.

Wolves sniff the breeze, searching for a scent
to locate the trouble.

Former students gather to mourn
their friend and professor.

Poets lower their standards,
read their poems out loud.

Ode to W.B. Yeats

What's it like to travel to a city
that honors its writers and artists?
To be in a place where there are
museums, galleries, libraries, and parks
that display these creators in photos,
posters, quotes from their writings,
bookshelves full of their works, and statues?

At the Yeats exhibit in the National Library
of Ireland, I took a selfie with a large poster that read,
"What will you find today?"
Then, another selfie with a life-sized photo
of Yeats with the two of us together like pals.

Down the street, I toured one of Yeats's homes
where he lived with family—
wife and two children—from 1922—1928.
After that, I walked to St Stephen's Green
to see an abstract sculpture of Yeats
done by Henry Moore.

Where had Maud Gonne go off to?
What happened to séances?
Was it Georgie Hyde-Lees and automatic writing
that made the difference?
Books of poems followed: *The Tower, The Winding
Stair,* and *A Full Moon in March.*
Poems: "Sailing to Byzantium," "Coole Park,"
"Parnell's Funeral."

Auden's "Ode to Yeats" said,
"Mad Ireland hurt you into poetry...,"
followed by "Earth receive an honorable guest:
          William Butler Yeats is laid to rest.

Let the Irish vessel lie
Emptied of its poetry."
Yet Yeats put these words on his headstone in Sligo,
"Cast a cold eye On Life, on death.
Horseman pass by."

Memorial

Three of us looked curiously
at W. S. Merwin.
Why had he asked us to take him
to the Bloedel Reserve?

We all stood now next to the guest house
and beside what had been a swimming pool.

Merwin recited poems that I didn't recognize
until he chanted "My Papa's Waltz" and
"Elegy for Jane."

One of us remembered that Theodore Roethke,
a guest of the Bloedel family,
had died in the then pool many years ago.
He whispered these facts to us as Merwin
continued his recitation, poem after poem
until he recited the last poem, "I knew a Woman."

This setting of elms, ferns, and flowers
must have appealed to Roethke
as it did now to Merwin.

Finally, we realized we were witnessing
Merwin's eulogy to Theodore Roethke's death.

My Wall of Writers

As I sat in St Stephen's Green among
the statues of Dublin's Prized writers,
including Yeats and Joyce,
I thought of my own experience in my study
where I sat before my computer,
working at editing and revising poems.
On one side of me, a wall filled with
framed photos of my favorite writers
that inspire me to continue to write.

Thomas Hardy is in the middle
above John Steinbeck,
the subject of my Ph.D. dissertation:
John Steinbeck: America's Isaiah.
On one side of these is W.B. Yeats,
and on the other, James Joyce.
On either side and below are Robert Frost,
Dylan Thomas, W.H. Auden, T.S. Eliot,
Pablo Neruda, Robert Lowell,
Wallace Stevens, and others.

How many times, when I have suffered
writer's block, have I pulled their books off
the shelves to read favorite poems!

Above and around these men are
some of my favorite women authors:
Elizabeth Bishop, Anna Akhmatova,
Jane Hirshfield, Joyce Carol Oates,
and Denise Levertov, women who brought
Pablo Neruda and W.B. Yeats into their own.

Muse

Just when I thought it was too late,
               you appeared.
Your charms, selfless and provoking,
               sent me waltzing.
You offered words and rhythms
               without demands.
You drew me down pages
               with preferred measures.

I followed faithfully, across
               open spaces.
At times my rhymes faltered,
               imagination failed.
But I danced to your meter,
               counting two by two.

Then you were gone,
               abrupt as a period.
Perhaps you went to give your attentions
               to another.

I will wait, visit poets you've courted,
read aloud their words and verses,
yield only to future embraces
               from you.

Sculpting Words

Once a poet said to me
"How can you address yourself
to a piece of wood?"

I replied, "Wood keeps its shape
after pieces are chipped away.
Words are slippery,
subject to context,
nuance, and connotation.
Just write the word father,
you'll know what I mean."

A sculptor carves precise form,
hopes his wood won't check,
causing cracks in proportions.
As he molds and finishes,
he works with the grain—
polishing against abrasions.

I return to words,
begin again the search for image,
metaphor, rhythm, and language—
to make life wonderous
in all its complications,
trying to get it right, just for me.

My Wild Prairie Rose

Once a carpet dealer in Istanbul
offered me 200 camels for you.
An inheritor of trading savvy
since the Silk Road days,
he saw what I knew of your value.

Where does your joy come from?
You flip open the cell phone, greet your caller,
break into laughter with eyes sparkling,
dance through questions and answers.

Where does your courage come from?
You married me, a college student of twenty,
gave birth to our son and daughter,
taught feisty pupils for years in three States,
cruised with your amateur captain to Desolation Sound,
snorkeled in Maui, biked the STP,
hiked into the Valley of Silent Men,
traveled with your guide to Granada, Rome, Berlin,
toured to Zion, Alexandria, St. Petersburg and Cartagena.

A farmer's daughter,
the eighth and last child,
born on the sand hills of North Dakota,
in a four seasoned climate
of spring rains, summer heat, long cool autumns,
and longer winters with howling winds,
blizzards and sub-zero weather,
in a culture of prescribed chores—
milking cows, plucking eggs from hens,
doing dishes for combining crews,
in close view of nature—

a bull with heifers in pasture,
cows calving in barns,
hissing geese in the farmyard,
and coyotes howling in the night—

you learned what was real,
what it is to work,
how to survive with your share,
and to receive and return love.
No dream could offer more!

Acknowledgments

My gratitude to the editors and publishers of the following presses and journals where these poems appeared or are forthcoming, often in earlier versions.

Cirque Journal: "Way of Life or Love?"

Crab Walk Press: "Andalusia"

Evening Street Review: "My Wild Prairie Rose"

Laughing Cypess, Inc. (American Pen Women, Seattle Branch): "Earth Map"

Natural Affinities (MoonPath Press, 2017): "My Sister Veronica," "Hitchhiking," "Danger on the Slopes," "Key West, Florida," "Departure in 1893," "In Memory of William Stafford," and "Denise Levertov"

Paper Boat Journal: "# 658."

Poets West Journal: "Acoma Pueblo."

My gratitude also to the editors of the following books which are sources of many views by authors on dreams in their writings:
Familiar Quotations: Editor, John Bartlett.
Writers Dreaming: Editor, Naomi Epel.

In addition, this book by Epel is one source for the title of this collection, *Dream World*.

Also I want to thank Nancy Rekow and Kris Hotchkiss for their suggestions about editing and revision of this manuscript. Both are poets who live, write, and help others with their writing on Bainbridge Island.

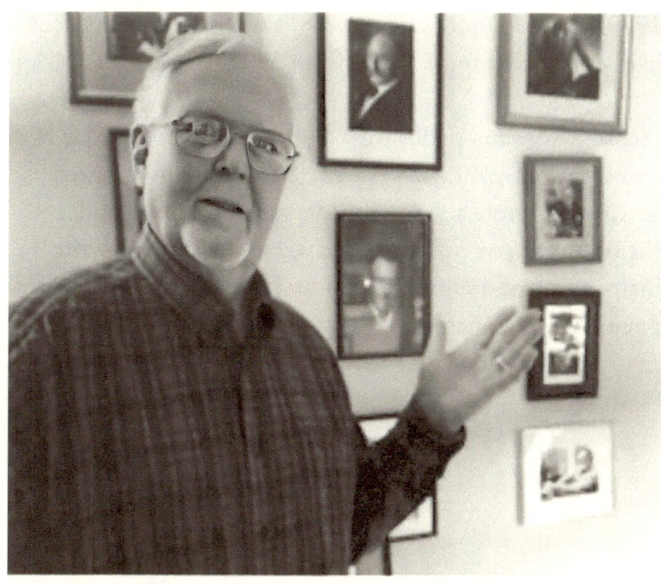

About the Author

David Hecker has been reading, teaching and writing poetry for many, many years. This practice has been his salvation in response to the many difficulties that all of us face in life. He has had many of his poems printed in journals over the past years, but most importantly was the publication of his first book of poems, *Natural Affinities*, by MoonPath Press in 2017. Within one month of the publication, Garrison Keillor read one of the poems "Hitchhiking" on his *Writers Almanac* broadcast. In 2018, another poem in the collection, "In Memory of William Stafford," was nominated for a Pushcart Prize.

Hecker earned a BA in English at Minot State Teachers College, an MA in English Education at the University of Minnesota, and a Ph.D. in American Studies at Washington State University. In his life as professor and writer, Hecker was selected as a Washington State Centennial Scholar in

1989. He co-founded and directed a writers' conference for five years at Olympic College from 1992–1996.

Hecker wrote and published a memoir titled *Full Circle: A Journey in Search of Roots* (2012) that details his ancestry. In 2014, he wrote and published a historical novel under the title *Strangers Before the Bench*. He continues to write many poems and submit to various journals. The most recent poems are published or forth-coming from *Cirque* and *Evening Street Press*.